7 SEVEN KEY STEPS TO SUCCESS

By

Noel A. Weiland

COPYRIGHT

Table of content

INTRODUCTION

Success can be broadly defined as achieving a desired outcome or goal. However, what constitutes success can vary greatly depending on the individual, their values, and their goals.

For some people, success may be measured by achieving financial wealth, while for others it may be measured by making a positive impact in their community or in the world. Some may see success as achieving personal growth or reaching a certain level of expertise in a particular field, while others may define it in terms of their relationships with loved ones or their overall level of happiness and fulfillment.

Ultimately, success is subjective and can be defined in many different ways. It is up to each individual to determine what success means to them and to work towards achieving their own personal goals and aspirations.

The story of Max

Once upon a time, there was a young man named Max who had always struggled with school. Despite his best efforts, he never seemed to be able to keep up with his classmates and always received poor grades. Max's teachers and parents tried to help him, but nothing seemed to work.

As Max grew older, he became more and more discouraged. He felt like a failure and began to lose confidence in himself. He started to believe that he would never be able to succeed in life.

One day, Max's best friend introduced him to a mentor who had been through similar struggles in the past. The mentor shared his own story of overcoming failure and achieving success, which inspired Max to try again.

Max began to focus on his strengths and work on his weaknesses. He spent long hours studying and practicing, determined to prove himself. At first, it was difficult and he made many mistakes, but he kept pushing forward.

Over time, Max began to see improvement in his grades and his confidence grew. He started to believe that he could achieve his goals and began to set new ones for himself. He also started to surround himself with positive and supportive people who believed in him.

Years went by, and Max's hard work and dedication paid off. He graduated with honors from college and went on to start his own successful business. He was able to inspire others who had struggled like him and became a mentor to those who needed guidance.

Max realized that his failure in school had been a blessing in disguise, as it had taught him the importance of perseverance, hard work, and determination. He was grateful for the struggles he had faced and the lessons he had learned along the way.

And so, Max's story became one of moving from failure to success, proving that with the right mindset and support, anyone can achieve their dreams.

CHAPTER ONE: SETTING SMART GOALS

When it comes to achieving success, setting goals is one of the most important things you can do. However, not all goals are created equal. To be truly effective, goals need to be SMART – specific, measurable, achievable, relevant, and time-bound. In this chapter, we'll explore how setting SMART goals can help you achieve success in all areas of your life.

Specific Goals

The first element of SMART goals is that they are specific. This means that they are clear and well-defined. When you set a specific goal, you know exactly what you want to achieve and what you need to do to get there.

For example, instead of setting a vague goal like "get fit," you might set a specific goal like "run a 5K race in under 30 minutes." This goal is specific because it clearly defines what you want to achieve and how you will measure your success.

Measurable Goals

The second element of SMART goals is that they are measurable. This means that you can track your progress and measure your success.

Using the previous example of running a 5K race, you might track your progress by recording how far you run each day, how long it takes you to run a mile, and how your body feels after each run. By measuring your progress, you can see how far you've come and adjust your approach if necessary.

Achievable Goals

The third element of SMART goals is that they are achievable. This means that they are challenging but realistic. Setting goals that are too difficult or unrealistic can lead to frustration and disappointment.

When setting achievable goals, it's important to consider your current level of ability and the resources you have available. For example, if you've never run before, it might be unrealistic to set a goal of running a marathon in six months. A more achievable goal might be to run a 5K race in three months.

Relevant Goals

The fourth element of SMART goals is that they are relevant. This means that they are aligned with your values, passions, and overall vision for your life.

When setting relevant goals, it's important to consider why you want to achieve them. For example, if you're setting a fitness goal, ask yourself why it's important to you. Is it because you want to improve your health, feel more confident, or set a positive example for your children? By understanding the underlying motivations behind your goals, you can stay motivated and committed even when the going gets tough.

Time-Bound Goals

The fifth and final element of SMART goals is that they are time-bound. This means that they have a specific deadline or timeframe for completion.

Having a deadline helps to create a sense of urgency and can help you stay focused and motivated. Without a deadline, it's easy to procrastinate and put off taking action.

For example, if you set a goal of running a 5K race in three months, you might break that goal down into smaller, time-bound milestones. You might aim to run one mile without stopping within the first month, run two miles within the second month, and run the full 5K race within the third month.

How SMART Goals Help with Achieving Success

Now that we've covered the five elements of SMART goals, let's explore how setting SMART goals can help you achieve success in all areas of your life.

Clarity

Setting specific goals helps to bring clarity to your vision for your life. When you know exactly what you want to achieve and why, you can create a roadmap for getting there.

Motivation
Having measurable goals helps to keep you motivated. When you can see progress and measure your success, it's easier to stay committed and focused.

Focus
Setting achievable goals helps to create focus. By breaking down larger goals into smaller, achievable milestones, you can stay focused on the steps you need to take to achieve your ultimate goal.

Prioritization
Setting relevant goals helps you prioritize your time and energy. When your goals are aligned with your values and passions, you're more likely to invest your time and energy in them.

Accountability

Setting time-bound goals helps to create accountability. When you have a deadline for completing a goal, you're more likely to take action and stay committed.

Adaptability

Setting SMART goals allows for adaptability. As you track your progress and measure your success, you can adjust your approach if necessary. If you're not making progress towards your goal, you can reevaluate your approach and make changes to ensure that you're on track.

Success

Ultimately, setting SMART goals helps you achieve success. When you have a clear vision, stay motivated and focused, prioritize your time and energy, and hold yourself accountable, you're more likely to achieve your goals and experience success in all areas of your life.

Examples of SMART Goals

Here are some examples of SMART goals to help inspire you in setting your own goals:

Career Goal: Obtain a promotion within my current company within the next six months by completing three professional development courses and exceeding my performance targets.

Financial Goal: Save $10,000 in the next 12 months by creating a monthly budget and reducing unnecessary expenses.

Fitness Goal: Complete a half marathon in six months by running four times per week and increasing my distance by 10% each week.

Personal Development Goal: Read 12 books within the next year by dedicating 30 minutes each day to reading and tracking my progress using a reading log.

Relationship Goal: Strengthen my relationship with my partner by having a weekly date night and practicing active listening skills during our conversations.

In conclusion, setting SMART goals is a powerful tool for achieving success in all areas of your life. By setting specific, measurable, achievable, relevant, and time-bound goals, you can bring clarity to your vision, stay motivated and focused, prioritize your time and energy, hold yourself accountable, and achieve your goals. So, take some time to reflect on your own goals and how you can make them SMART. With the right mindset and approach, you can achieve anything you set your mind to

CHAPTER TWO: DEVELOPING AN ACTION PLAN

Setting goals is an essential step towards achieving success, but it's not enough on its own. Once you've set your goals, the next step is to develop a plan of action to achieve them. A plan of action provides a roadmap for achieving your goals and helps you stay focused and motivated throughout the journey.

In this chapter, we'll discuss how developing a plan of action can help you achieve success and the key steps you can take to create an effective plan.

Why Develop a Plan of Action?

- **Provides Clarity**

Developing a plan of action helps you gain clarity about what needs to be done to achieve your goals. It breaks down your goals into smaller, actionable steps, making it easier to understand what you need to do to get there.

- **Sets Priorities**

A plan of action helps you prioritize your tasks and focus on the most important ones. It allows you to allocate your time and resources effectively, making it more likely that you'll achieve your goals within the desired timeframe.

- **Keeps You Accountable**

Developing a plan of action creates a sense of accountability. When you have a clear roadmap of what you need to do to achieve your goals, you're more likely to take action and stay committed. It also makes it easier to track your progress and make adjustments as necessary.

- **Increases Motivation**

Having a plan of action in place can increase your motivation and confidence. It provides a sense of direction and purpose, and seeing progress towards your goals can be highly motivating.

- **Improves Focus**

A plan of action helps you stay focused on what's important. It reduces the chances of getting distracted by other tasks and activities, and helps you stay on track towards your goals.

Steps to Developing a Plan of Action

- **Identify Your Goals**

The first step in developing a plan of action is to identify your goals. These should be specific, measurable, achievable, relevant, and time-bound (SMART) goals. Once you've identified your goals, break them down into smaller, actionable steps.

- **Determine Your Resources**

Determine what resources you have available to help you achieve your goals. This could include time, money, knowledge, skills, and support from others. Consider what resources you need to acquire and how you can obtain them.

- **Create a Timeline**

Create a timeline for achieving your goals. Break down your goals into smaller milestones and determine when you want to achieve each one. This will help you stay on track and ensure that you're making progress towards your goals.

- **Determine Your Action Steps**

Determine the specific actions you need to take to achieve each milestone. These actions should be specific, measurable, achievable, relevant, and time-bound. Consider what obstacles you may face and how you can overcome them.

- **Monitor Your Progress**

Regularly monitor your progress towards achieving your goals. This will help you stay on track and make adjustments as necessary. Consider using a planner, a journal, or a project management tool to help you stay organized and track your progress.

- **Adjust Your Plan**

Be prepared to adjust your plan as necessary. If you encounter unexpected obstacles or if your circumstances change, you may need to revise your plan. Remain flexible and open to new ideas and approaches.

Examples of Developing a Plan of Action

Here are some examples of how developing a plan of action can help you achieve success:

1. **Career Goal**: To obtain a promotion within my current company within the next year. Identify the specific skills and qualifications needed for the promotion. Determine the steps needed to acquire those skills and qualifications, such as taking courses or attending conferences. Set a timeline for completing each step. Monitor progress towards each milestone and make adjustments as necessary.

2. **Financial Goal:** To save $10,000 for a down payment on a house within the next two years.
    Determine the monthly savings needed to reach the goal.
    Identify arcas where expenses can be reduced to increase savings.
    Set a timeline for achieving savings milestones.
    Monitor progress towards each milestone and adjust expenses and savings as necessary.

3. **Health Goal**: To lose 20 pounds within the next six months.
   Determine the specific actions needed to achieve the goal, such as exercising for 30 minutes a day or reducing daily calorie intake.
   Set a timeline for achieving weight loss milestones.
   Monitor progress towards each milestone and adjust actions and habits as necessary.

4. **Business Goal**: To increase sales by 20% within the next year.
   Identify the specific marketing strategies needed to achieve the goal, such as increasing online presence or expanding customer base.
   Determine the steps needed to implement those strategies, such as developing a social media campaign or networking with potential customers.
   Set a timeline for implementing each strategy and achieving sales milestones.

Monitor progress towards each milestone and adjust strategies as necessary.

Developing a plan of action is an essential step towards achieving success. It provides clarity, sets priorities, keeps you accountable, increases motivation, and improves focus. By identifying your goals, determining your resources, creating a timeline, determining your action steps, monitoring your progress, and adjusting your plan as necessary, you can create an effective plan of action that will help you achieve your goals.

Remember that success is not just about setting goals, but also about taking action towards achieving them. Developing a plan of action is a key step in that process, and it can make all the difference between success and failure. So take the time to develop a plan of action for your goals, and start taking action towards achieving them today.

CHAPTER THREE: STAYING FOCUSED AND MOTIVATED

Staying focused and motivated is an essential element for achieving success. It is not only about setting goals but also about staying determined and committed to achieving them. Successful people are not born with an innate ability to focus and motivate themselves; they have learned and cultivated these traits over time. In this chapter, we will explore the importance of staying focused and motivated in achieving success and some strategies to help you develop these traits.

The Importance of Staying Focused:

Focus is the ability to concentrate your attention and energy on one task or goal without getting distracted by other things. Staying focused is crucial for success because it helps you:

Enhance Productivity:

When you are focused on one task, you can accomplish it more efficiently and effectively. Multitasking, on the other hand, can decrease productivity and lead to more errors.

Improve Decision-Making:
When you are focused on your goals, you can make better decisions. You can evaluate the pros and cons of different options and choose the best course of action.

Increase Creativity:
Focused thinking can help you generate new ideas and solutions. When you are not distracted, your brain can make connections and see patterns that might not be apparent otherwise.

Build Resilience:
Staying focused requires discipline and persistence. By developing these traits, you can become more resilient and better able to cope with setbacks and obstacles.

Strategies for Staying Focused:

1. **Set Clear Goals**:
   Having clear goals can help you stay focused on what you want to achieve. Make sure your goals are specific, measurable, attainable, relevant, and time-bound. Write them down and review them regularly.

2. **Minimize Distractions**:
   Distractions can disrupt your focus and decrease your productivity. Some common distractions include social media, email, and notifications. To minimize distractions, turn off your phone, close unnecessary tabs on your computer, and work in a quiet environment.

3. **Use Time Management Techniques**:
   Effective time management can help you stay focused on your goals. Techniques such as the Pomodoro technique, which involves working for 25 minutes and then taking a short break, can help you stay on task and avoid burnout.

4. **Take Breaks:**
    Taking breaks can help you recharge and refocus. Instead of working for hours on end, take short breaks every hour or so. During your break, do something relaxing, such as taking a walk or meditating.

The Importance of Staying Motivated:

Motivation is the drive and energy that propels you towards your goals. Staying motivated is crucial for success because it helps you:

Overcome Obstacles:
Motivation can help you overcome obstacles and challenges. When you are motivated, you are more likely to persist in the face of setbacks and keep working towards your goals.

Stay Committed:
Motivation can help you stay committed to your goals. When you are motivated, you are more likely to stick to your plan and not give up when things get tough.

Improve Performance:
Motivation can improve your performance. When you are motivated, you are more focused and engaged in your work, which can lead to better results.

Increase Satisfaction:
Motivation can increase your satisfaction with your work and life. When you are motivated, you are more likely to feel a sense of purpose and fulfillment.

Strategies for Staying Motivated:

1. **Find Your Why**:
   Understanding why you want to achieve your goals can help you stay motivated. Take some time to reflect on your values and what drives you. Write down your why and refer to it when you need a boost of motivation.

2. **Celebrate Small Wins**:
   Celebrating small wins can help you stay motivated. When you achieve a milestone, take the time to acknowledge

your progress and give yourself a pat on the back. This can help you stay motivated and energized for the next phase of your journey.

3. **Surround Yourself with Supportive People:**
   Surrounding yourself with supportive people can help you stay motivated. Choose people who believe in you and your goals and who can provide encouragement and support when you need it.

4. **Visualize Success**:
   Visualizing success can help you stay motivated. Take some time each day to visualize yourself achieving your goals. Imagine how it will feel to accomplish your goals and what your life will be like once you achieve them.

Staying focused and motivated is critical for achieving success. By developing these traits and using the strategies outlined in this article, you can improve your productivity, decision-making, creativity, resilience, performance, and satisfaction. Remember that staying focused and motivated is not always easy, and there will be times when you feel like giving up. However, by staying committed and persistent, you can overcome obstacles and achieve your goals. Keep in mind that success is not just about reaching the destination; it's about enjoying the journey and growing along the way.

CHAPTER FOUR: TAKING ACTION

The pursuit of success is a universal aspiration that everyone desires. However, achieving success requires more than just wishing and dreaming about it. It demands deliberate actions, hard work, and perseverance. Taking action towards your goals is essential to achieve success. When you take action, you create momentum, and momentum creates progress. Progress, in turn, breeds more progress, and before you know it, you've achieved your goals. In this chapter, we will explore how taking action and making progress towards your goals can help you achieve success.

The Importance of Taking Action:

Taking action is the first step towards achieving your goals. It is one thing to set goals and another thing entirely to take action towards achieving them. Without action, goals remain mere wishes or fantasies. Taking action is the bridge between where you are now and where you want to be. It involves moving from your comfort zone, overcoming fear and uncertainty, and doing something that brings you closer to your goals. The importance of taking action towards your goals cannot be overstated. Here are some reasons why:

- **Action breeds momentum:** Taking action creates momentum, and momentum leads to progress. When you take action, you build momentum, and that momentum propels you forward, making it easier to take more action towards your goals.

- **Action breeds confidence:** Taking action towards your goals builds your confidence. When you take action, you begin to see progress, and that progress gives you the confidence to take even more action towards your goals.

- **Action leads to results**: Taking action is the only way to achieve results. Without action, you cannot achieve anything. When you take action towards your goals, you create the conditions for success.

- **Action builds resilience**: Taking action involves overcoming obstacles and challenges. These challenges build resilience and prepare you for future challenges that may arise.

The Benefits of Making Progress:

Making progress towards your goals is a critical component of achieving success. Progress is the fuel that keeps you motivated and inspired. When you make progress towards your goals, you feel a sense of accomplishment and satisfaction. Here are some benefits of making progress towards your goals:

- **Progress increases motivation**: Making progress towards your goals increases your motivation. When you see progress, you feel motivated to keep going and to achieve even more.

- **Progress provides feedback**: Making progress towards your goals provides feedback on what is working and what needs to be improved. This feedback helps you to adjust your strategy and approach to achieve your goals.

- **Progress builds confidence:** Making progress towards your goals builds your confidence. When you see progress, you believe in yourself and your ability to achieve your goals.

- **Progress leads to momentum**: Making progress creates momentum, and momentum leads to even more progress. When you make progress towards your goals, you build momentum that makes it easier to achieve even more.

How Taking Action and Making Progress Lead to Success:

Taking action and making progress towards your goals are critical ingredients for success. When you take action towards your goals, you create momentum, and that momentum leads to progress. Progress, in turn, builds motivation, confidence, and resilience. Here are some ways taking action and making progress towards your goals can help you achieve success:

Clarity: Taking action towards your goals brings clarity. When you take action, you learn more about your goals, your strengths, weaknesses, and what needs to be improved.

Focus: Taking action towards your goals helps you to focus. When you take action, you eliminate distractions and focus on what is essential.

Discipline: Taking action towards your goals requires discipline. When you take action, you develop discipline that helps you to stay focused and motivated.

Consistency: Taking action towards your goals requires consistency. When you take action consistently, you build momentum that makes it easier to stay consistent.

Growth: Taking action and making progress towards your goals helps you to grow. When you take action, you stretch yourself, learn new things, and develop new skills.

Resilience: Taking action and making progress towards your goals helps you to develop resilience. When you face obstacles and challenges, you learn to overcome them, and that resilience prepares you for future challenges.

Achievement: Taking action and making progress towards your goals leads to achievement. When you achieve your goals, you feel a sense of accomplishment and satisfaction.

Self-mastery: Taking action and making progress towards your goals helps you to master yourself. When you take action, you learn to control your thoughts, emotions, and actions.

How to Take Action and Make Progress Towards Your Goals:

Taking action and making progress towards your goals may seem overwhelming at first.

However, with the right mindset, approach, and strategies, you can achieve success. Here are some tips on how to take action and make progress towards your goals:

Set SMART Goals: Set goals that are Specific, Measurable, Achievable, Relevant, and Time-bound. SMART goals help you to focus, plan, and track progress towards your goals.

Develop an Action Plan: Develop an action plan that outlines the steps you need to take to achieve your goals. Your action plan should be realistic, achievable, and flexible.

Prioritize: Prioritize your actions based on what is most important and what will have the most significant impact on achieving your goals.

Take Consistent Action: Take action consistently, even if it is a small action. Consistent action builds momentum and leads to progress.

Track Progress: Track your progress towards your goals regularly. Tracking progress helps you to stay motivated, adjust your approach, and celebrate successes.

Stay Accountable: Stay accountable to yourself and others. Share your goals with someone who can support and hold you accountable for taking action and making progress towards your goals.

Taking action and making progress towards your goals is essential to achieve success. When you take action, you create momentum that leads to progress, motivation, confidence, and resilience. Making progress towards your goals provides feedback, builds confidence, increases motivation, and creates momentum that makes it easier to achieve even more. By setting SMART goals, developing an action plan, prioritizing, taking consistent action, tracking progress, and staying accountable, you can take action and make progress towards your goals, leading to success. Remember, success is not a destination, but a journey that requires taking action, making progress, and enjoying the process.

CHAPTER FIVE: LEARN FROM YOUR MISTAKES

Learning from your mistakes is one of the most important aspects of achieving success. Mistakes are a natural part of the learning process, and they allow us to grow and develop in ways that would not be possible without them. However, it is not enough to simply make mistakes – we must also learn from them and make adjustments accordingly. In this chapter, we will explore how learning from your mistakes and making adjustments can help you achieve success in all areas of your life.

First and foremost, it is important to understand that making mistakes is not a sign of weakness or incompetence. On the contrary, mistakes are a necessary part of the learning process, and they can provide valuable insights into how we can improve and grow. Whether we are learning a new skill, pursuing a new career, or simply trying to improve our relationships, mistakes are inevitable but they are also opportunities for growth and development.

One of the key benefits of learning from your mistakes is that it allows you to identify areas where you need to improve. When we make mistakes, we are forced to confront our limitations and weaknesses, and this can be a humbling experience. However, by acknowledging our mistakes and taking steps to address them, we can become better equipped to overcome obstacles and achieve our goals.

Another benefit of learning from your mistakes is that it helps you develop resilience and perseverance. When things don't go as planned, it can be easy to become discouraged and give up. However, by learning from our mistakes and making adjustments, we can develop the resilience and perseverance we need to keep going, even in the face of setbacks and obstacles.

In addition to these benefits, learning from your mistakes can also help you develop a growth mindset. A growth mindset is the belief that our abilities and intelligence can be developed over time, rather than being fixed traits that we are born with. By learning from our mistakes and making adjustments, we can develop a growth mindset that allows us to approach challenges with a sense of curiosity and a willingness to learn.

So how can we learn from our mistakes and make adjustments? Here are a few strategies to consider:

- Take responsibility for your mistakes. It can be tempting to blame others or external factors for our mistakes, but this only prevents us from learning and growing. Instead, take responsibility for your mistakes and focus on what you can do differently in the future.

- Reflect on your mistakes. After making a mistake, take some time to reflect on what went wrong and why. This can help you identify areas where you need to improve and develop a plan for how to make adjustments.

- Seek feedback from others. Sometimes it can be difficult to see our own mistakes and limitations. By seeking feedback from others, we can gain valuable insights into how we can improve and grow.

- Make a plan for how to make adjustments. Once you have identified areas where you need to improve, make a plan for how to make adjustments. This could involve setting specific goals, seeking out additional training or support, or changing your approach to a particular task or situation.

- Practice, practice, practice. Learning from your mistakes and making adjustments requires consistent effort and practice. By committing to regular practice and seeking out opportunities for growth and development, you can achieve success in all areas of your life.

Lastly, learning from your mistakes and making adjustments is an essential part of achieving success. Mistakes are inevitable, but they provide valuable opportunities for growth and development. By taking responsibility for your mistakes, reflecting on what went wrong, seeking feedback from others, making a plan for how to make adjustments, and committing to consistent practice, you can overcome obstacles and achieve your goals. So don't be afraid to make mistakes – embrace them as opportunities to learn and grow, and you will be on your way to success in no time.

CHAPTER SIX: CELEBRATING YOUR SUCCESS AND STAYING COMMITTED

Success is a subjective term that can mean different things to different people. For some, success may mean achieving financial stability, while for others, it may mean finding fulfillment in their personal relationships or career. Whatever your definition of success may be, one thing is certain – it requires a significant amount of hard work, determination, and commitment. In this chapter, we will discuss how celebrating your successes and staying committed can help you achieve success in any area of your life.

The Power of Celebrating Your Successes

Celebrating your successes is an essential aspect of achieving success. It may seem counterintuitive to take a break and celebrate your achievements when you still have a long way to go, but it can actually be a powerful motivator to keep pushing forward.

When you celebrate your successes, you acknowledge the progress you've made and remind yourself of what you're capable of achieving. It gives you a sense of accomplishment and boosts your self-esteem, which can have a positive impact on your overall well-being.

Celebrating your successes doesn't have to be grandiose or expensive. It can be as simple as taking a day off to relax and do something you enjoy, treating yourself to your favorite meal or activity, or sharing your achievements with loved ones. The important thing is to take the time to acknowledge your accomplishments and recognize the hard work you've put in.

Staying Committed to Your Goals

Commitment is another critical factor in achieving success. It's easy to start working towards a goal, but it's much harder to stay committed and see it through to the end. Whether you're trying to lose weight, start a new business, or learn a new skill, staying committed is crucial to achieving success.

Here are some tips on how to stay committed to your goals:

Define Your Goals Clearly: Make sure you have a clear understanding of what you want to achieve and why it's important to you. This will help you stay motivated and focused on your goals.

Develop a Plan: Break down your goals into smaller, achievable steps and create a plan to help you stay on track. This will make your goals feel less daunting and more manageable.

Hold Yourself Accountable: Take responsibility for your actions and hold yourself accountable for your progress. This will help you stay motivated and ensure that you're making progress towards your goals.

Find a Support System: Surround yourself with people who support and encourage you. This could be friends, family members, or a coach or mentor who can provide guidance and motivation.

Stay Positive: Focus on the progress you've made and the steps you've taken towards your goals, rather than dwelling on any setbacks or obstacles. A positive mindset will help you stay motivated and committed.

The Benefits of Celebrating Your Successes and Staying Committed

Celebrating your successes and staying committed to your goals can have numerous benefits, both personally and professionally. Here are some of the benefits you can expect:

Increased Motivation: Celebrating your successes and staying committed can boost your motivation and help you stay focused on your goals. This can help you overcome any obstacles or setbacks and keep pushing forward.

Improved Confidence: Celebrating your successes can boost your confidence and self-esteem, making you feel more capable of achieving your goals. Staying committed can also improve your confidence by demonstrating your ability to follow through on your commitments.

Greater Resilience: Celebrating your successes and staying committed can help you develop greater resilience and perseverance. This can help you bounce back from setbacks and stay focused on your goals, even in the face of adversity.

Enhanced Productivity: Staying committed to your goals can increase your productivity and efficiency, as you'll be more focused and less likely to be distracted. Celebrating your successes can also increase your productivity by boosting your morale and motivation.

Improved Relationships: Celebrating your successes can help strengthen your relationships with loved ones by giving them an opportunity to share in your accomplishments. Staying committed can also improve your relationships by demonstrating your reliability and commitment to others.

Greater Satisfaction: Celebrating your successes and staying committed can lead to greater satisfaction and happiness in your personal and professional life. Achieving your goals can give you a sense of purpose and fulfillment, which can lead to a more meaningful and satisfying life.

Achieving success requires a combination of hard work, determination, and commitment. Celebrating your successes and staying committed to your goals are two key factors that can help you achieve success in any area of your life. By taking the time to acknowledge your accomplishments and stay focused on your goals, you can increase your motivation, confidence, and resilience, leading to greater satisfaction and happiness. So, take a moment to celebrate your successes and stay committed to your goals – the rewards are sure to follow.

CHAPTER SEVEN: CONTINUOUSLY IMPROVING AND GROWING

Success is not a destination; it is a journey that requires continuous improvement and growth. Whether you're trying to improve your skills, advance your career, or achieve personal goals, a commitment to ongoing improvement and growth is essential. In this article, we will discuss how continuously improving and growing can help you achieve success in any area of your life.

The Benefits of Continuous Improvement and Growth

Continuous improvement and growth are not just buzzwords; they are essential components of achieving succcss. Here are some of the benefits you can expect:

Increased Competence: By continuously improving and growing, you can become more skilled and knowledgeable in your chosen field. This can increase your competence and confidence, making you more valuable to employers and clients.

Improved Efficiency: Continuously improving and growing can help you become more efficient and productive. This can save you time and effort, enabling you to achieve more in less time.

Greater Innovation: By constantly seeking new knowledge and ideas, you can become more innovative and creative. This can help you stay ahead of the competition and identify new opportunities for growth and success.

Enhanced Reputation: Continuous improvement and growth can enhance your reputation and credibility in your field. This can increase your visibility and attract new opportunities and clients.

Increased Satisfaction: Continuously improving and growing can lead to greater satisfaction and fulfillment in your personal and professional life. It can give you a sense of purpose and accomplishment, leading to a more meaningful and satisfying life.

Strategies for Continuous Improvement and Growth

Continuous improvement and growth require a commitment to ongoing learning and development. Here are some strategies to help you achieve this:

Set Goals: Set specific, measurable, achievable, relevant, and time-bound (SMART) goals to guide your efforts. This will help you stay focused and motivated, and measure your progress along the way.

Seek Feedback: Seek feedback from colleagues, mentors, or coaches to help you identify areas for improvement and growth. This can help you understand your strengths and weaknesses and develop a plan for improvement.

Attend Trainings and Conferences: Attend training programs and conferences to learn new skills, gain new insights, and network with other professionals in your field.

Read Books and Articles: Read books and articles on topics related to your field to stay informed and up-to-date. This can help you gain new knowledge and ideas and enhance your skills and competencies.

Engage in Self-Reflection: Engage in self-reflection to assess your progress and identify areas for improvement. This can help you develop self-awareness and make more informed decisions.

Embrace Challenges: Embrace challenges and seek out new experiences that stretch your abilities and enable you to grow. This can help you develop resilience and adaptability, which are essential traits for success.

The Importance of a Growth Mindset

Having a growth mindset is essential for continuous improvement and growth. A growth mindset is the belief that abilities and intelligence can be developed through hard work, effort, and dedication. It contrasts with a fixed mindset, which is the belief that abilities and intelligence are innate and unchangeable.

A growth mindset enables you to embrace challenges, learn from failure, and persist in the face of setbacks. It also helps you stay open to new ideas and perspectives, enabling you to continuously improve and grow.

Here are some strategies for developing a growth mindset:

Embrace Failure: Embrace failure as an opportunity to learn and grow, rather than a reflection of your abilities. View mistakes as a natural part of the learning process and focus on what you can learn from them.

Practice Gratitude: Practice gratitude by focusing on what you have achieved and the progress you have made, rather than dwelling on what you havent yet accomplished. Gratitude can help you maintain a positive outlook and increase your resilience in the face of challenges.

Challenge Your Assumptions: Challenge your assumptions and beliefs about yourself and your abilities. Be open to new ideas and perspectives, and seek out feedback from others to help you identify blind spots and areas for improvement.

Cultivate a Learning Mindset: Cultivate a learning mindset by approaching every experience as an opportunity to learn and grow. Stay curious and ask questions, and seek out opportunities to expand your knowledge and skills.

Practice Self-Compassion: Practice self-compassion by treating yourself with kindness and understanding, especially when facing setbacks or challenges. Recognize that growth and improvement are a process, and be patient and supportive of yourself along the way.

Continuous improvement and growth are essential components of achieving success in any area of your life. By setting goals, seeking feedback, attending trainings and conferences, reading books and articles, engaging in self-reflection, embracing challenges, and cultivating a growth mindset, you can continuously improve and grow, leading to increased competence, efficiency, innovation, reputation, and satisfaction.

Success is not a destination; it is a journey that requires a commitment to ongoing learning and development. By embracing this journey and staying committed to your personal and professional growth, you can achieve success and create a fulfilling and meaningful life.

www.ingramcontent.com/pod-product-compliance
Lightning Source LLC
Chambersburg PA
CBHW071112220526
45467CB00004B/1821